JOURNEYS IN ART

J.D. Lewis

CHERRYTREE BOOKS

A Cherrytree Book

Designed and produced by Touchstone Publishing Ltd
Gissing's Farm, Fressingfield, Eye, Suffolk IP21 5SH, England
and 33 Cromford Road, London SW18 1NZ, England

First published in 1996 by Cherrytree Press Ltd
a subsidiary of The Chivers Company Ltd, Windsor Bridge Road
Bath, Avon BA2 3AX, England

Copyright © Cherrytree Press Ltd 1996

Editor: Louisa Somerville
Designer: David Armitage
Cover designer: Tim Peters
Artwork: Annabel Spenceley

Cover picture: *Colonel James Todd travelling by elephant through Rajasthan with
his cavalry and sepoys*, Anon

British Library Cataloguing in Publication Data
Lewis, J.D.
    Journeys in Art. – (In Art Series)
    I. Title II. Series
    704.94

    ISBN 0-7451-5265-1

Printed and bound in Italy by STIGE

Contents

In every chapter of this book you will find a number of coloured panels. Each one has a symbol at the top to tell you what type of panel it is.

Activity panel Ideas for projects that will give you an insight into the techniques of the artists in this book. Try your hand at painting, sculpting and crafts.

Information panel Detailed explanations of particular aspects of the text, or in-depth information on an artist or work of art.

Look and See panel Suggestions for some close observation, using this book, the library, art galleries, and the art and architecture in your area

Setting out

Setting off on a journey can be very exciting. It might be a holiday to somewhere we have never been before or the chance to live or work in a new place. Wherever the destination, a journey involves change. Sometimes it's just a change of place, but often a journey involves a change in our feelings, too. As well as feeling excited, we may be anxious about what lies ahead, and sad about those people we leave behind. Our feelings also vary depending on the type of journey and how long we will be away. A soldier leaving for war and a person going on holiday will experience different emotions, but both

will be involved in fond farewells.

These moments of departure have always been popular as subjects for artists. Sometimes an artist will want to make a record of what happened, but often the purpose of the painting is to capture the emotions not only of those who are going, but also of the ones left behind. It's a moment that we all find fascinating – look in any newspaper and you will probably find photographs of departures. Take a look at the pictures in this chapter. Have the artists tried to show you what the people in their paintings are feeling? This will depend on when and where the artist lived.

Into the wilderness

In 15th-century Europe, there were few books for people to read. They learned about the Christian story from pictures and sermons. Priests and bishops paid artists to paint pictures for their churches. These paintings had to be clear and easily understood. Artists painted haloes around the heads of saints so that they could be distinguished from ordinary people.

◄ John the Baptist leaves the gateway of his town and sets off for the barren rocky landscape of the desert to prepare himself for his new life as a prophet. There are two figures in the painting, but both are John the Baptist. The artist has combined two episodes of the story in one picture, rather like a comic strip. Although the houses get smaller as they get further away, the prophet himself stays the same size – perhaps because of his importance in the story. Does John look ready for a long journey? Why do you think he has so few provisions for life in the desert?
[St John the Baptist retiring to the desert, *Giovanni di Paolo*]

Departure art
Have you noticed that old main railway stations are often quite grand? The Victorians, who built the first railways in Britain, were very proud of this new means of transport. They made many of their stations look like cathedrals, with decorative ironwork and stonework. Have a look at a departure point near where you live – a bus station, a harbour or an airport, for example. Have the architects included some kind of decoration? If not, have any pictures, sculpture or special lettering been added?

Giovanni di Paolo, an Italian artist, was commissioned to paint an altarpiece showing the life of John the Baptist, the cousin of Jesus. John's mission in life was to tell people about Jesus and prepare them for baptism. Before he started his work, he went into the desert to fast and pray. He lived on locusts, wild honey and nothing else. The picture on page 4 shows John the Baptist at his moment of departure. People who saw this painting in the church were inspired by the story of a man giving up home comforts for the sake of his beliefs.

To a new world

John the Baptist is a solitary, determined figure as he sets off on his journey. In the picture below, by the 19th-century British artist Ford Madox Brown, the people are much less confident about their departure. The family are leaving home for a new life overseas. Life was hard for many people in Britain at this time. Opportunities for making a better life existed on the other side of the world, but moving from home and family was a wrench, and who knew what the future would hold?

Busy places

While Brown conveys the private feelings of two individuals setting off on a

◀ *The two people in this painting certainly look unhappy about setting off on their journey. They are turning away from the famous White Cliffs of Dover, England, and heading off for a new country. The young woman holds the hand of a small child under her grey cloak. With her other hand she holds on to her husband for comfort. The strong wind blowing the woman's scarf suggests there will be a long, uncomfortable journey ahead.*
[The Last of England, 1852, *Ford Madox Brown*]

▲ *Everything in this busy railway station seems to be moving. The artist has painted many of the people with a brush loaded with paint, then outlined them in a strong black line. Delaney's technique captures an atmosphere full of frenzied activity and tension. A seething mass of figures twists and turns under the high arches of the station building. The soldiers await their trains, watched by a military policeman, but few others take notice of them. They have their own lives to lead, shoes to be cleaned, time to kill, trains to catch.*
[Penn Station During Wartime, 1943, *Joseph Delaney*]

long and difficult journey, the painting above by the American artist Joseph Delaney takes a broader view of a scene that is equally charged with emotion. In 1943 thousands of American soldiers joined the allied forces fighting World War II in Europe. Those who were departing had their minds full of the dangers ahead of them, but for everyone else, life was continuing as usual. Delaney captures the frenzied atmosphere of the moment of the forces' departure from the railway station.

Journey to truth

There is no sense of tension in the Indian carving on page 8, which shows the departure of a prince from his palace. This prince was the first Buddha, revered by all who follow the Buddhist faith.

Prince Siddhartha Gautama grew up in a palace,

surrounded by luxury. When he was 29 years old, he cut off his hair, exchanged his princely clothes with those of a poor man and went on a journey in search of truth. He travelled for many years, meditating and fasting for long periods of time.

On his 35th birthday Siddhartha came to a place called Bodh Gaya. Here he sat on a grass mat under a tree and meditated until he reached the state that Buddhists describe as 'fully enlightened'. At this point he became the first Buddha and has been honoured ever since. Incidents in his life have been the subject of many paintings and sculptures.

Relief carving

The Amaravati carving of Prince Siddhartha's departure is known as a relief sculpture. Relief sculpture is not free-standing. Part of the stone, wood or other material from which it is carved provides a background to the scene. There are several types of relief sculpture. Their names indicate the depth of the carving.

High relief is a sculpture that is almost completely detached from its background.

Low relief sculpture projects less far from the background. It is often called bas-relief ('bas' is French for low). Intaglio is relief in reverse. This means that the carved design is sunk into the surface of the material, rather than projecting from it.

▼ *This carving is 2000 years old. It shows the departure of Prince Siddhartha from his palace in search of truth. His faithful servant leads him on his stately horse. Mythical creatures lift up the horses' hooves to ensure a quiet departure. Dancing gods and spirits express their joy at Siddhartha's decision to go. This scene is part of a frieze that surrounds a huge Buddhist shrine in Amaravati, India. It was carved from big slabs of limestone, a soft stone good for making fine detail and sharp edges. Limestone can easily be damaged, so it is fortunate that the frieze is in such good condition. [Renunciation, Amaravati carving]*

Departure tiles

Make your own departure scene on a series of clay tiles. You could work with a group of friends and make one tile each.

What you need
- paper and pencil
- 3 or 4 balls of self-hardening clay about the size of a tennis ball.
- rolling pin and a piece of old canvas or sacking to stop the clay sticking to the work top
- two strips of wood about 1cm thick and 40cm long, for guide sticks
- small pot of water
- piece of card 12cm x 12cm and an old blunt knife
- modelling tools

What you do

1 Decide on your scene. It could show yourself or someone you know, or it could be a scene from a story. On a piece of paper draw pencil lines to mark out a series of squares in a grid pattern or in a row. Then sketch out your scene. Make sure each square has a part of the picture in it.

2 Put the guide sticks 20cm apart. Roll out a ball of clay with the rolling pin until it looks like a flat piece of pastry. Keep turning the clay a quarter turn or it will spread over the guide sticks. Stop when the rolling pin is rolling on the sticks and not making the clay any thinner.

3 Put your square card in the centre of the clay and cut round it with an old, blunt knife. You now have a soft clay tile that you have to handle gently.

4 Repeat steps 2 and 3 to make as many tiles as you wish. You will have to work out how the scene on one tile links up with the scene on the next.

5 Make the figures and the scenery out of clay.

6 To stick the figures and scenery on the tile,

dip your finger in water, wet the surfaces and press the parts together. Press firmly or the parts will separate when the clay dries out.

7 Use a modelling tool to carve out background relief shapes in the tile.

8 When you have finished modelling and carving let your tiles dry out very slowly.

9 Use poster paints to colour your departure scene.

 # 2 On the road

Except for the fortunate few, travel has always been arduous, uncomfortable and sometimes dangerous. Before engines were invented, people had to travel overland with pack animals.

Nomadic art

Nomadic people do not have fixed homes. They live in dwellings that can be moved, such as tents or caravans. This means that their art also has to be portable. The nomadic peoples of Asia developed the art of weaving on simple hand looms. These could be assembled quickly wherever they happened to be. They used the wool from their animals and dyes from local plants to make intricately patterned carpets and shawls that could be rolled up and carried from place to place.

◄ *This finely modelled camel wears a harness and a very haughty expression. How has the artist made the animal appear so proud? Do you think it is a realistic portrayal of the animal?*
[Chinese pottery model of a standing camel, T'ang dynasty]

China from China

In the Far East, two-humped camels from Mongolia and Turkestan enabled travellers to cross the cold, rocky deserts and mountain trails. These Bactrian camels could carry packs for long distances without water.

Like many other ancient civilizations, the Chinese made everyday items from pottery. By the time of the T'ang dynasty (AD 618-907), they had started to make decorative items too. Chinese pottery was of such high quality that people took to calling the finest pottery 'china',

a name that we still use today.

Because the camel was so important to the Chinese, and perhaps because the animal is such a distinctive shape, it was often represented in Chinese art.

Travel by elephant

In India the poor have always walked from place to place. High above them, in days long past, their resplendent rulers rode on the backs of stately elephants. Later the British went to India to trade, and they stayed to found an empire, protected by the British army. The senior officers joined Indian princes on the backs of the elephants.

The picture on page 11 shows a British colonel and a group of Indian sepoys (soldiers). The picture is a miniature. It is painted in vibrant colours and has a great feeling of movement. The artist has flattered his subject, by placing him high up in the centre of the picture. All the other figures display respect and look up to him.

Road to the races

In western countries, the horse was the usual beast of burden. Horses were used for all kinds of work, including pulling fashionable coaches or humble wagons. The people in the picture below are on the way to Epsom Downs, in southern England, for an annual horse race called the Derby. People from all over the country would make their way to the race course to enjoy themselves.

In this picture the artist Thomas Rowlandson exaggerates the overcrowding on the road to the race course. Rowlandson liked to draw people doing ordinary things

▼ *We see this scene as if we, too, are journeying along the road behind all the wagons and horses. The crowds and the chaos show how much discomfort we are prepared to endure for the sake of a good day out. Rowlandson's picture is a lithograph – a special kind of print. The drawing was made on a very smooth block of stone and a large number of prints were taken from it.* [On the road to Epsom, *Thomas Rowlandson*]

▼ *The artist has deliberately made the people in this picture look too big for their cars. Both drivers and passengers look as if they are turning into monsters and they are heading straight for us. It could be a nightmare!* [Driver, *1973, Sieghard Gille*]

and looking slightly ridiculous. He appreciated the humour in the chaos of people trying to get to the races.

The nightmare of travel

These days the roads to Epsom on Derby Day are still packed with traffic, but today the people are in cars, isolated from each other. People become frustrated by delays and traffic jams and tend to get angry and aggressive.

Sieghard Gille lives and works in Germany. In his painting on this page, he shows car travellers as horrific creatures – cut off from each other in their cars, but herded together on the road, united by their aggressive expressions and grotesque appearance. His drivers are threatening.

The people that George Segal creates in his life-size sets are also cut off from each other. To make his models, he covers real people in plaster bandages. He allows these to dry then cuts them off, lets the people out and joins up the plaster casts.

Look at his *Bus Riders* on page 14. His commuters look more ordinary than Gille's monster-travellers but they also look lifeless, like Egyptian mummies, embalmed for the journey to the afterlife (see page 43). Segal makes us feel that when we travel on public transport we are not really living.

▼ *These figures are plaster-casts of real people sitting on real bus seats. But they do not look real; the white plaster drains all semblance of life from them. Next time you travel by bus see if your fellow passengers look at all like this.*
[Bus Riders, *1962, George Segal*]

Many people take a camera with them when they go on holiday. Why not make some drawings instead? All you need is a sketchpad, one 2B pencil and a sharpener (or black felt-tips). Make drawings of some of the things that you see around you. Try close-ups of details as well as views. You could stick some of your drawings on blank cards and send them to friends or relations. They will be appreciated much more than a conventional picture postcard.

Watercolour technique

The Indian picture on page 11 was painted with watercolour. Watercolour paints are useful to take with you on a journey or on holiday because they don't take up much room in your luggage. However, many people get frustrated using watercolour because one shape often bleeds or dribbles into another. Here is a technique to avoid this problem.

What you need

- tin of watercolour paints and a pot of water. You could use blocks of tempera colour if you do not have watercolour
- pencil and two springy watercolour brushes (eg, No. 6 and No. 10)
- some small pieces of thick white paper
- piece of board and some sticky tape
- old rag or some tissues

What you do

1 Tape a piece of paper to the board. Work on a table with the board tilted towards you.
2 Draw some shapes lightly on the paper with a pencil. You could make these forms of transport – a car, a plane or a camel.
3 Now dip your brush in the water and wet the background only. Start with your larger brush at the top and work across and down, moving the big dribble of water gradually to the bottom of the paper. Brush the water carefully to the edges of your shapes.
4 With a brush full of colour start at the top and let the colour flood down and over the paper. Recharge your brush if necessary. Keep the tip of your brush well away from the dry shapes.
5 When the paper is quite dry, you can use the same technique to wet your shapes and colour those in the same way. The colour will not run into the outside area.
6 Once the base colour is dry, you can paint other colours over the top.
7 When you have practised these techniques, try painting a picture of a form of transport in a landscape.

 # Pioneers and explorers

We know little about the earliest explorers. Some people believe that the ancient Egyptians crossed the Atlantic Ocean to America, but we have no hard evidence for this. If they did, they must have been exceedingly brave. At the time, people believed that the world was flat and that anyone travelling too far would fall over the edge.

The Vikings

The Vikings were not afraid of travelling too far. They were passionate adventurers and skilful sailors. From their homeland in what we now call Scandinavia, they explored and raided many of the coastal areas of western Europe and reached inland areas by sailing up the rivers. In their insatiable quest for land and wealth, they sailed across the Atlantic Ocean as far as Canada.

Viking longships were works of genius. Not only were they elegant to look at, they were also perfectly designed to cope with the stormy conditions of the North Atlantic. The bow and stern of a boat were often decorated with carved animals or monsters. They were intended to frighten away bad spirits, but they must also have scared human enemies. Much Viking carving was characterized by ornate, curved patterns, seen also in their gold and silver jewellery. Other carvings depicted scenes from Viking legends.

▼ *Some Viking kings were buried in their ships. This dragon was discovered at the site of a ship burial ground, in a position where it would guard the body of the king from evil spirits. It is carved from a tall wooden post. Notice how the patterns weave through each other, as though the wood itself has come alive.* [Carved dragon-head post from Oseberg Ship Burial]

▶ *Trade with China gave Europe a taste for tea. This watercolour, painted in about 1800 by an unknown Chinese artist, shows bales of tea from the countryside being taken downstream on rafts to a port for export to the West. Look at the landscape, the figures and the building. How can you tell that this place might be in China? The tea was grown on high ground. Can you see how the artist has indicated (and exaggerated) this point?* [Transporting tea downriver to Canton]

Trade with the East

During the Middle Ages, Venice was one of the world's great trading cities. In 1262, a young man named Marco Polo set off with his merchant father to travel through Persia (now Iran) and on into China. Marco Polo stayed in China for 17 years. He learned to drink tea and eat noodles. He watched silk being produced and books being printed. He described these and other experiences in a book on China, which inspired other Europeans to develop their trade with the East.

The long overland route across Asia was used more

Wood carving
To carve as well as the Vikings you have to know a lot about wood. All wood has a grain, and it is much easier to shape when you cut along the grain rather than across it.

Some wood is more suitable for fine carving because it is softer and the grain is very close and dense. Lime is excellent for carving delicate and intricate work, but it is not very durable and is best used for work kept indoors.

For carvings that have to stand outside, a harder wood must be used, such as oak, walnut or mahogany. To carve a figurehead for a ship you would need a very large tree trunk.

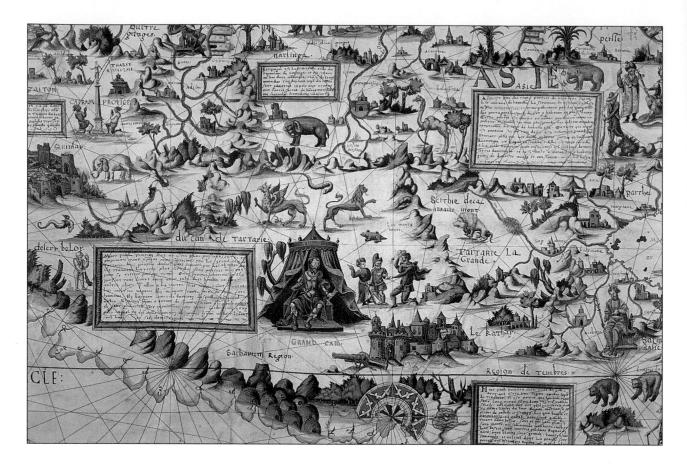

and more, and became known as the Silk Road. Goods from the East, including fine porcelain, silk and other textiles, were transported to the West by camels and other animals. These beautiful artefacts were highly prized, and both western and eastern artists were inspired by the exotic peoples they met and by the strange new activities they observed.

As new parts of the world were discovered, it became necessary to draw maps. Based on travellers' tales, these were not accurate route maps, for map makers had no reliable means of measuring the land. The maps were usually decorated with pictures of whatever might be seen on the road. The map on this page was based on Marco Polo's own account of his journey from Moscow to Persia.

Pioneers of the Wild West

During the 19th century, Europeans emigrated to America in huge numbers. They left poverty and

▲ *This beautiful old map is more like a series of pictures. Is is based on an account written by Marco Polo and shows his route from Moscow to Persia. It would not be much help in finding the route, but it gives you some idea of what Marco Polo saw on his journey. Notice the elephants. Would you expect to see them in this part of the world nowadays? [Jenkinson's map, engraved in 1562]*

▲ *The grand scale of this picture shows the importance of the opening up of the American West. Benton felt very strongly about the dignity of ordinary men and women, and he has positioned his figures carefully to make them look important. The doorway has been used to make the figures look as if they really are conquering and overcoming all the difficulties. Below the main picture is another, showing the journey of the wagon trains.* [Independence and the opening of the West, *Thomas Hart Benton*]

persecution and sought a better life in the New World. When they reached the east coast cities, many continued their journey by wagon train to the west. Some were unable to survive the harsh weather and treacherous terrain; others were killed by Native Americans, angered that strangers were stealing their land.

The stories of the west became like the myths and legends of earlier times. Many artists painted exciting scenes of cowboys rounding up cattle, of battles with native people, and of the wild

landscape. The heroic, pioneering (and sometimes exaggerated) stories were particularly suitable for large-scale paintings.

Thomas Hart Benton, a 20th-century artist, painted murals (wall paintings) in public places to celebrate national events and inspire patriotic feeling. The mural on this page shows the pioneers and the people they met on their journey.

Today film makers tell the stories of American heroes and show the landscapes of the Wild West on huge cinema screens.

▼ *This poster captures the excitement of the pioneer days. It includes a picture of the Northern Pacific train, and advertises the frontier towns of Dakota and Montana in an attempt to attract adventurous customers. Every part of the poster is filled with the names and pictures of the places that the train visits. The lettering itself provides an important decorative effect. How many different kinds of lettering have been used?*
[*Northern Pacific Railroad advertisement*]

There are many different sorts of maps: street maps, tourist maps, cycling maps, walking maps and road maps for the car. There are maps of subway or overground railways, and the water companies even have maps of their drains and water supply pipes. Look at a selection of such maps and compare them. What is the same about them, and what is different? Note whether they look like a plan (like a subway map) or are more pictorial (like a tourist map). In what ways are they well adapted for their particular purpose?

Plan a park

The map on page 18 uses small pictures to describe Marco Polo's route. Draw this kind of map of a park or recreation area near you. If there isn't one, here's your chance to design your ideal recreation area! Illustrate the different sections with pictures of what you might see on a walk through the park. There may not be elephants and camels, but there will probably be dogs and ducks. You may find an outline plan to help you at the entrance to the park.

What you need
• paper or sketch book
• soft pencil
• pastels

What you do
1 Get permission to go to a local park with a friend. Walk round it and sketch a plan. Note the different areas for dog-walking, playing ball games, tennis courts, flower gardens and trees. If you are designing your ideal recreation area, base your plan on some open space near you.
2 At home, turn your plan into an illustrated drawing or painting, so that anyone looking at your map would know exactly what to expect on a visit to your recreation area.

4 Legendary journeys

◄ *This drinking cup shows the Greek hero Jason being rescued by the goddess Athene from the mouth of the dragon guarding the Golden Fleece. The fleece hangs on a tree in the background. See how skilfully the artist has fitted the figures into the circle. The lines and shapes all flow around Jason's head, which is in the centre of the cup.*
[Jason being regurgitated by a serpent, *Athenian red drinking cup*]

Almost every culture in the world has its own myths and legends, stories about gods and goddesses, fantastic beasts and superhuman heroes. These tales were passed down from generation to generation by word of mouth. They helped to explain the mysteries of the real world and gave people something to believe in and admire.

Many of the stories tell of epic journeys, or quests, made by heroes who performed extraordinary feats. For thousands of years, these stories have been the subjects of much of the world's art. Even though we now know that the stories were mostly imagined, they continue to fascinate us. They are retold in books and in films and in recent years they have even been adapted as computer and video games.

Look in your local library for art books showing scenes from legendary journeys. Try to work out how the artist has made the heroes important. Have they been painted in different colours or painted larger than other figures in the painting perhaps?

Wandering Greeks

The ancient Greeks were a nation of seafarers, so it is not surprising that their myths frequently included journeys by sea. Odysseus and Jason were two great legendary heroes who had to travel the seas and face trials and difficulties. They often needed the help of friendly gods and goddesses.

Jason and the Golden Fleece

One day, Jason set out from Thessaly in Greece for Colchis on the Black Sea. His mission was to bring back the Golden Fleece of a ram, which was nailed to a tree and guarded by an unsleeping dragon. If he could return with this he would become king of Thessaly.

Jason's journey was made in the *Argo*, a boat with 50 oars – one for each of the crew, who were known as the Argonauts. After many adventures, he reached Colchis, where Medea, the king's sorceress daughter, fell in love with him. Using magic powers she helped him capture the Golden Fleece, and together they returned to Thessaly.

Red figures

Greek artists loved to decorate their pottery with episodes from the stories of Jason, Odysseus and other heroes. For a long period, it was customary to decorate black vases with red figures. The figures were painted with a liquid made from clay and black wood ash. This turned red when it was fired in the kiln. The artist had to paint the figures before the red clay got too dry. Fine brushes were used to create graceful flowing lines. The pot was fired only after it was completely dry.

A famous general

Jason and Odysseus probably never existed, but Alexander the Great was real enough. As a boy he was inspired by the old Greek stories, and grew up to be brave and ambitious. Alexander became king when he was only 20 years old, after his father, King Philip of Macedonia, was murdered. He led the Greek armies to the borders of India and established the largest empire in the ancient world. It included Egypt, Asia Minor, Persia, Afghanistan and part of India.

Handmade books

Our libraries today are full of printed books like the one you are reading now. But before the days of printing, stories were written out by hand and the pictures painted by artists. The example in this chapter is from a Persian manuscript, but handmade books were also made in Europe. Many were hand-lettered by monks.

Apart from the Church, only kings, princes and the really wealthy could afford to pay for all the valuable materials and craftsmanship required to make a book. Cow, calf, sheep or goat skins were cleaned and stretched and made into parchment, ready for writing on. The person who did the writing was called a scribe. He used a quill pen and was skilled in calligraphy, the art of beautiful handwriting. The illuminator, or illustrator, worked with a fine brush to apply bright colour, and gold or silver leaf to the illustrations. A variety of powdered pigments was used for the colours. These were mixed with egg yolk to help the colours stick to the parchment. The most expensive colour was a rich blue, made from a blue stone called lapis lazuli. It was more valuable than the gold!

The scribe and illuminator worked on loose sheets before the book was finally bound.

Because they were so precious, few people were allowed to see these books.

▲ *Alexander the Great is dressed in green and wearing a crown. Newly arrived in India, he is encountering all sorts of exotic people and animals. Do you think the men in the boat are trying to* scare away the sea monster *while they tie up their boat – or are they trying to fish the creature out of the water?* [Alexander the Great before a Hindu Idol, *Persian manuscript*]

Many great paintings and sculptures of Alexander and his exploits were created during his lifetime and for centuries afterwards. The illustration on this page is taken from a Persian book about him, written 2000 years after his death.

Bible stories

The Bible describes many important journeys: Moses leading the Jewish people out of Egypt; the journey to Bethlehem; the flight of Joseph, Mary and the infant Jesus into Egypt; the travels of St Paul; the journey of the Magi to Bethlehem.

A magus (plural magi) is a wise man. The Magi in the Bible story are usually known as the three kings, or wise men. Perhaps they were astronomers following the path of a comet. No one knows who they really were, but tradition says that they travelled a great distance to pay homage to the infant Jesus and to present him with gifts of gold, frankincense and myrrh. The story has always been popular with artists.

Benozzo Gozzoli lived 500 years ago in the city of Florence, Italy. He painted many murals which could be seen on public display in Italian cities. In those days Florence was a rich city. It was famous for its processions and pageants in which the ruling families dressed in splendid clothes and paraded before the ordinary people of the town. The painting below

▶ *One of the three kings sets off from his castle to travel the winding road to Bethlehem. The artist has not included the traditional star for the king and his royal companions to follow across a desert landscape. The painting tells us more about life in Florence where the artist lived than it does about the lands of the Bible and the religious story. Two of the nobles have found some time for hunting – a popular pastime in 15th-century Florence. The citizens who saw this painting would have appreciated all the gold, splendour and richness of this scene.*
[Journey of the Magi to Bethlehem, *Benozzo Gozzoli*]

shows one of the three kings on his way to Bethlehem. In this traditional story, Gozzoli saw a perfect opportunity to combine a religious theme with a demonstration of the pomp and ceremony that the city loved so much.

As the crow flies

According to the Shinto religion, the ancestors of the Japanese emperor were gods. The first emperor was called Jimmu-tenno. Aided by a magic sword and guided by a crow sent down from heaven, Jimmu-tenno travelled north from his home in Kyushu, through Honshu to Yamata. There he built a palace and settled down to rule his new empire.

The picture of Jimmu-tenno on this page is a wood-block print. To make it, the artist drew the picture on paper. A craftsman then copied the picture several times on to finer paper, and pasted the copies on to as many blocks as there were colours.

On each block the craftsman then gouged out all the wood around the parts of the picture that were to be a particular colour, and left only those

parts raised. The block was coated with the colour and paper pressed on it, so that the ink was transferred to the paper.

As soon as it was dry, it was pressed on to another block with another part of the picture on it. In this way the print was built up layer by layer. This method of printing is different from that used by Shiko Munakata (see page 29).

▼ *Jimmu-tenno puts fear into the hearts of his enemies as he sets out on his journey of conquest, guided by the black crow, which leads him safely across the stretch of water between the islands of Kyushu and Honshu. The creature's divine origins are shown by the rays of light that fill the background.* [Jimmu-tenno sets out on his journey east, *Tsukioka Yoshitoshi*]

Design and paint a mural

Find a place at home or school where you can put up a mural. Paint your mural on to paper first, then ask permission to stick your mural to a wall. Where would a mural look good? What about a school corridor or your room at home?

What you need

- supply of paper, one piece 40cm x 20cm, 16 pieces 100cm x 50cm, specially cut
- paint, brushes, water, charcoal, pastels, pencils, coloured pencils
- long rule, short rule

What you do

1 To make a finished mural 4 metres x 2 metres, make your design 40cm x 20cm (one-tenth of the finished size).

2 Choose a famous journey you know of – ancient or modern – or make one up. Select one or more parts of it.

3 Draw your design on your small piece of paper. Use any suitable materials – paint, coloured pencils or computer graphics etc. Try not to make the shapes too complicated. Simple shapes are easier to enlarge.

4 Draw 3 faint vertical lines and 3 horizontal lines on your small design to divide it into 16 equal rectangles. (Each rectangle will be 10cm x 5cm.) This will help you transfer the design accurately to your larger sheets of paper.

5 Ask some friends to help you paint the large version. Take each rectangle from your small design and copy it carefully on to each of your 16 larger pieces of paper.

6 Join your 16 pieces of paper together at the back with sticky paper, making sure they are all in the right place. Now your mural is ready to hang.

Life's journeys

Writers often describe life as a journey, a physical and emotional one. As we grow older our bodies change, and so do our thoughts and feelings. We are on an intellectual and emotional journey from the moment we are born. Stages on this journey are often celebrated in art.

Becoming an adult

The journey from childhood to adulthood is celebrated in many cultures as a solemn moment, the point when a child takes on more duties and responsibilities and can be included in adult rites and rituals. Celebrations vary, but they usually include singing and dancing.

African masks

The men of the Bapende tribe, who live in central Africa, traditionally wore masks while the boys were initiated into the secrets of the tribe's religious lore. By wearing masks such as these, tribesmen were able to make contact with the spirits.

Far from home

Sometimes great changes occur in people's lives through no fault of their own. People say that their hearts are broken by the loss of loved ones, and by being away from their families. During World War II, many people were evacuated from cities to escape the bombing. Shiko Munakata, a Japanese print artist, was evacuated from his

▲ *Wearing a mask allows you to take on a different personality. The Bapende people make their masks from a number of different materials. The main part is carved from wood cut from the trees in the rain forest where they live. The hair or scarf is made from woven fabric and plaited pieces of fibrous plant.*
[Bapende initiation mask from Zaire]

home in Tokyo. He felt homesick and lonely. During this time he read some poetry about loneliness and made a series of woodcuts based on the poems.

Japanese prints

The Japanese word for a print is *hanga*. In the past the print was a very special Japanese art form. Munakata started painting in oils, but because he wanted his art to be Japanese rather than European, he decided to specialize in woodcut prints. He became very involved in Buddhism and his work became a religious activity for him.

To make his prints, he first cut lines and shapes into thin wooden blocks about 3 cm thick. Because he had bad eyesight he had to sit very close to his work. To take a print, he rubbed ink over the

▶ *This woodcut is mounted in a large screen with 30 other prints. The whole series is called 'Roaming Far From Home'. Part of this picture includes a poem about loneliness, written in Japanese characters that seem to fly across the bands of colour, like the large birds at the top. Munakata has tried to put his feelings into the shapes and colours of the prints. He describes the colour of the poet's sorrow as 'a little paler than the colour of the deep blue sea'. Japanese paper is very strong and transparent so that light shines through from behind, making the print glow.*
[The Colour of Sadness, *Shiko Munakata*]

Artists abroad

Like Gauguin, many artists travel to foreign countries for inspiration. Such a journey may change the way they paint, allowing them to use new colours and techniques. In the 16th and 17th centuries Rome was the art capital of the western world, and the city attracted large numbers of French, Flemish and Dutch painters who stayed and worked there, sometimes for years. Their work changed as it became influenced by the art they saw around them. The Flemish painter Peter Paul Rubens for example, started to paint his male figures in the style of the great Italian, Michelangelo. The French painter Nicolas Poussin was inspired by the splendour of ancient Rome, and his work is full of references to the classical world of the Romans.

In the 19th century the English artist J.M.W. Turner made several sketching tours in Europe. He used these as the basis for the large paintings he completed in his studio at home. One of Turner's paintings is on page 38.

The modern artist David Hockney moved from England to live in Los Angeles, where he has been inspired by the light, the architecture and the lifestyle. Some of his most memorable pictures are of swimming pools, painted not long after his arrival in the United States.

board, then lowered thin Japanese paper on to it and rubbed the back of it with a special pad wrapped in bamboo, called a baren. In this way the print was transferred from the wooden block to the paper.

Munakata was always experimenting with different ways of printing. He sometimes used a brush and coloured his prints from behind. He then put them on screens and allowed the light to reveal the colours through the paper.

Travelling artists

When we say we have had a 'change of heart', it means we feel differently about something. Sometimes people change their whole lives as a result of a change of heart. The painter Paul Gauguin gave up working in a bank because he wanted to be a painter. Later in his life he left his home in France and spent ten years in the South Sea islands of Tahiti and the Marquesas. He discovered a wonderful paradise of beautiful people living in an exotic landscape. Gauguin felt that these simple people were in touch with a spiritual

▶ *The title of this picture, Arearea, is a Polynesian word meaning joyfulness. Maybe it reflects the artist's feelings about his new life in this sunny and relaxed South Sea island. Two young women sit under a tree. One plays a flute while the other looks towards us. In the foreground a dog gently sniffs the grass, while in the distance some figures are worshipping an idol. Everything here is calm. The simple shapes are filled with dark glowing colours which help create the mood of the picture. Would you say that the colours are realistic? [Arearea, Paul Gauguin]*

world which had been lost to his contemporaries in France. His Tahitian paintings show an unhurried, peaceful life, but their dark, glowing colours have a moody and melancholy feeling. He would never have painted these pictures if he had stayed in France.

The road to Damascus

There are times when a change of heart can be very dramatic. The artist Caravaggio, who lived 400 years ago in Rome, specialized in painting particularly dramatic moments. One of these was *The Conversion of St Paul*. St Paul had persecuted any Jews who became Christians. One day on his way to Damascus he 'saw the light' – he had a vision of the risen Christ. Blinded and dumbstruck by the experience, he fell from his horse. He spent the rest of his life travelling the world as a missionary for Christ.

When you look at paintings, check the location of the scene and the nationality of the artist to see if the artist had painted the scene abroad. How far did the artist travel from his or her native land? Look for the date of the painting. How would the artist have travelled to this destination?

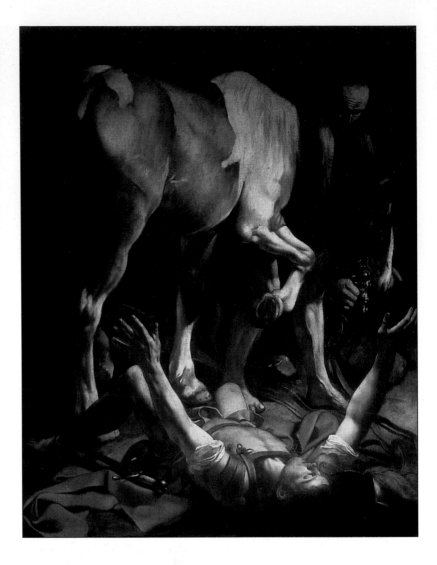

In the picture Paul looks as if he has just been attacked. An element of violence is often present in Caravaggio's work. The painter himself was frequently involved in fights. On one occasion he killed a man, and had to flee Rome to work in another part of Italy. Though it may seem strange that a murderer should paint religious pictures, his experiences seem to have benefited his art.

Maximum impact

Caravaggio used different techniques to make the maximum emotional impact. His figures, for instance, are often reaching out with their arms. And he was one of the first painters to use harsh light and deep shadows. He always used rough, ordinary people to depict religious events.

▲ *Paul, blinded by the bright light, lies where he has fallen. We look down on him from behind as he lies in the pool of light, his arms stretched up to heaven in ecstasy. The uncomprehending groom and the huge horse fill up more than half the painting. There is nowhere to move. This lack of space and the surrounding darkness make the picture claustrophobic and rather frightening.*
[Conversion of St Paul, Michelangelo Merisi da Caravaggio]

Many of his contemporaries were outraged by this, and by the violence of his work, but for us his paintings have an immediate emotional appeal.

Make a collograph

A collograph is a picture made up of pieces of paper or other materials, from which a print can be taken. (The word colle is the French word for glue.) The result looks very much like a woodcut. Try making a collograph of a journey that changed your life – a holiday, maybe, or your first day at school. Or it could be an inner 'journey' – perhaps a dream where something dramatic happens. This collograph shows a person dreaming that they are flying.

What you need
- two pieces of thin card about 25cm x 25cm
- printing roller and waterproof palette (eg, old piece of Formica)
- black, water-based printing ink
- old tablespoon and a small craft knife
- thin white paper and glue
- sheets of newspaper
- cutting board

What you do
1 Draw your picture in very simple shapes on one of the pieces of thin card.
2 Protect the table with newspaper and the cutting board, and cut out the shapes with the craft knife.
3 Arrange the cut-out pieces on your other piece of card and stick them down.
4 Stick down additional shapes to improve your picture. You could also draw into it with a ball-point pen. This will also print.
5 Roll out a small amount of ink on the palette. When you have a thin, even amount on your roller, roll it smoothly and steadily in all directions on your card. Do this three or four times, recharging your roller with ink each time.
6 Place your cardblock face up on a clean piece of newspaper. Put the thin white paper on top and burnish it with a spoon. You do this by pressing down the back of the spoon on to every part of the white paper and moving the spoon around in small circles as if you were polishing it.
7 Peel off the print. Look to see whether you need to add or take out anything. You may need some practice before you get the perfect print.

6 Journey's end

How do you feel when you get home from school? Happy? Relieved? Coming home makes most people feel happy, especially if they have been wretched while they were away or are bursting with excitement to tell some good news. Arriving in a strange place far from home makes people feel anxious and sad, unless they can be sure of a welcome.

Sharing joy

A Bible story, known as the Visitation, tells of a journey Mary made to visit her cousin Elizabeth, to let her know the good news that Mary was pregnant. She was expecting the infant Jesus. Elizabeth was much older and had been hoping to have a baby for many years. She was ecstatically happy because she too was now expecting a baby.

The Visitation was a popular subject in Christian art from the earliest times. All the paintings show Mary at the end of her journey, being warmly greeted by her cousin, but over the centuries this

scene was depicted in many different ways. At one time artists showed the two babies inside their mother's wombs, as if their paintings were X-ray photographs. Later on the story was shown in a more lifelike way, with the two women bowing to each other.

34

◄ *Mary, pregnant with the infant Jesus, visits her cousin Elizabeth, who is also pregnant, although Raphael has not made this so obvious. The babies can be seen in the sky with God, waiting to be born. The future relationship of the two boys is shown on the left of the painting. Elizabeth's son, John (the Baptist), is baptizing Mary's son, Jesus.*
[The Visitation, *Raphael of Urbino*]

Sometimes there were references to Mary's journey: a mule or some other form of transport was included in the painting.

Raphael lived in Italy about 500 years ago, when the Church was rich and powerful. He gained a reputation for painting Mary as a modest, graceful and devout young girl. He was in great demand to paint altarpieces for churches. One of these is the version of the Visitation that appears on the opposite page. In it, Raphael shows Mary demurely showing her pregnancy to Elizabeth.

Happy ending

The story of the Prodigal Son is another Bible story about a journey's end. The story is a parable – a Bible story that shows us how we should behave. Jesus told this parable to show how God will forgive us wrong acts if we are genuinely sorry.

The story tells how a father divided his wealth between his sons. The younger one left home and squandered his money. When he was destitute and miserable, he realized that he had been foolish, and returned home to ask his father's forgiveness. His

► *The Prodigal Son returns penniless from his carousing to the forgiving arms of his father. The old man holds his son's head lovingly in his lap while his other son looks on. The line drawing is sketched with a reed pen, but the surrounding areas are painted with a watery ink. It is the contrast of the light areas and shadows that creates the emotional atmosphere for the scene.*
[The Return of the Prodigal Son, *Rembrandt van Rijn*]

Drawing materials

To make a drawing, you only have to make a mark of some kind. Anything that can make a mark will do. Here are just a few of the many mark-making tools that artists have used.

Charcoal

Burnt sticks of wood were one of the very first drawing materials. Particularly favoured by artists today are burnt willow and burnt vine branches. Charcoal can be rubbed and smudged. It can make fine delicate lines as well as large areas of dense black.

Pencils

Pencils were first made in 1564 from graphite, a material mined in Cumberland, England. The graphite is mixed with clay to make it harder. Most pencils have the letters 'H' or 'B' and a number on them. H stands for hard. 4H or 5H pencils are extremely hard pencils that make a sharp light line. B stands for black. 5B or 6B pencils make a very black line because the graphite has little clay mixed with it. It also smudges easily.

Reed pens

Rembrandt liked to draw with pens made from the reeds found in ponds or lakes. The reed is carved into a nib at one end. The artist dips the nib into the ink and makes a mark on paper. A reed pen makes a very different line from a pencil line. When it is pressed down hard on the paper, the line becomes thicker and denser with ink. The ink line is sharper than a pencil line and of course it can't be rubbed out.

Quill pens

Quill pens are usually made from the feathers of geese or crows. They are long and flexible and can be cut thick or fine to make different widths of line. Rembrandt had three or four quills at hand. He often pressed very hard on them and made them blunt. Sometimes he used the other end to paint with.

Metal nib pens

These were first used in about 1748. A rigid nib is good for writing but a flexible nib is better for drawing. Often there is a split down the middle of the nib, allowing the artist to make a thicker line by pressing harder. Unless it is used in a fountain pen, a metal nib pen has to be dipped regularly in ink.

Brushes

Artists in China and Japan began using brushes for painting and writing over 2000 years ago. Paint brushes are usually made from animal hair fixed to a wooden handle. Stiff brushes are made from pig or goat hair, soft brushes from squirrel or rabbit. Nowdays many bristles are made from artificial fibres.

Fingers

Fingers are the simplest drawing tool and probably the one we all start with. Rembrandt frequently used his fingers, as have many other artists. As well as paint, all kinds of materials can be spread on a canvas by hand. Clays, chalks and other minerals are popular, as well as foods, and powdered wood mixed with plant juices.

father did not scold him because he was overjoyed to see his son again and knew that his son had seen the error of his ways. 'Your brother was dead,' he said to his other son, 'now he has come back to life. He was lost and is found.'

The story of the Prodigal Son appealed to the Dutch artist Rembrandt van Rijn because he loved his own son, Titus, so much. Rembrandt kept returning to the story again and again. For over 30 years he made etchings, drawings and paintings on this theme. Rembrandt was always drawing because it helped him to develop his ideas. He often used a reed pen, which few people use today (see opposite).

Exile and isolation

Ovid was a poet who lived in Rome about 2000 years ago. He was sociable and witty, and wrote poems about love, and the gods and other characters from Greek and Roman mythology. Then he offended the emperor and as a punishment he was exiled. His journey ended in a land he thought was barbaric, far away from Rome. He would have felt very lonely.

Eugène Delacroix, the 19th-century French artist who painted the picture below, sympathized with Ovid's situation. He enjoyed the good life in Paris and knew that people who loved city life, such as himself and Ovid, could never be happy away from sophisticated people and surroundings. In this way Delacroix was quite unlike Gauguin (see page 30), whose creative spirit was stimulated by the simple life in the South Seas.

▶ *The sophisticated Ovid has been exiled to a country far from Rome. The artist shows him lying in his luxurious blue and white robes, with scrolls at his side to be read or written on. His new neighbours bring him gifts or come to gaze on him out of curiosity. The big mare in the front of the picture is being milked – the people of this land drank mare's milk. Delacroix has painted Ovid in a beautiful, rugged landscape made even more intense with dreamy blues and reds. Despite the welcome from the Scythians, you can see that Ovid would feel lonely and out of place here, where no one would have read a line of his poetry.*
[Ovid among the Scythians, *Eugène Delacroix*]

The final journey

The English artist Joseph Mallord William Turner started young. When he was only nine he coloured some engravings for a local brewer, and he became a student at the Royal Academy School in London at 14. In the last chapter we saw how Turner went on a sketching journey through Italy. Turner wandered the British countryside, too, filling a traveller's notebook with precise drawings of landscape, castles and abbeys. These were so accurate that later they were engraved and used to illustrate travel books.

Turner grew up near the port of London. Here, as a young man in the early 1800s, he would see beautiful tall sailing ships from all over the world. He never lost his enthusiasm for painting ships and water, and he particularly enjoyed the hazards of sea travel. Once, during a storm at sea, he had himself tied to the mast of the ship. He could then draw the storm without fear of being washed overboard! Turner's love of ships and shipping is clear from his painting of *The Fighting Temeraire* (below). He records the last sad journey of the ship. She had a proud record of fighting in the Battle of Trafalgar, but here we see her being towed up the Thames to be broken up.

◄ *The elegant, ghost-like ship makes her final journey up the Thames. She is hauled by a powerful black tug, with fire belching from its funnel. The painting marks the end of an era: the great fighting ships have had their day. The glorious sky tells us what Turner feels. The ship ends its life in a blaze of glory as the sun sinks down to the horizon.*
[The Fighting Temeraire tugged to her last berth to be broken up, *J.M.W. Turner*]

Life drawing – arriving home

Many artists use models to pose for them while they draw a scene. For the Prodigal Son, Rembrandt dressed his models in costume. Draw someone arriving home, perhaps someone excited and happy or someone more wary of the welcome they will get.

What you need
- friend or family member
- dip pen and a bottle of ink *or* a thin black felt-tip pen
- some props – luggage or a school bag could be useful

What you do
1 Ask your model to pose for about half an hour as if they have just returned home from a journey. Pay special attention to your model's expression and stance. Ask them to look at something in particular, then they can move their head from time to time and return to the same position. Arms only have to be held out when you need to draw them! (Your model may need to rest after 15 minutes. Make sure to mark where they are standing before they move.)
2 While you are drawing your model, draw some parts of the room at the same time: the doorway maybe or part of the floor where they are standing.

3 When you have finished drawing the figure, your model can relax and you can spend as much time as you like drawing the other details in the room. You could include a dog or cat welcoming the person home.

The cycles of the Prodigal Son

In medieval Europe it was popular to depict the various stages of the story of the Prodigal Son in stained glass. It was called a 'cycle' because the journey of the younger son ended where it began. There could be four or more scenes. For example:
1 The son leaving home.
2 His feasting with women and spending all his money.
3 Being poor and earning his keep by looking after pigs.
4 Returning to the arms of his father and being forgiven.

Journeys of the soul

Life after death?

What do you think happens to us when we die? Do you believe in heaven and hell? Five hundred years ago most people in Europe were Christian. They were taught that there is a heaven and a hell and that on judgement day they would go to one or the other, depending on how good they had been. Life was more difficult than it is today and people usually died young, because of war and disease. They believed that their fate lay in God's

► *This terrifying painting shows St Anthony's vision of hell. It was part of the altarpiece that was painted for the chapel of a hospital where the monks of the order of St Anthony cared for the sick and dying. St Anthony – the patron saint of monks – is seen being tortured by the foul demons who inhabit hell. In the bottom corner is another suffering soul. His sores show us that he has the plague, and he too is going through the agonies that many people of Grünewald's time feared. God's help is on the way, however. He is in the golden glow in the sky and has sent his angels to fight the demons.*
[The Isenheim Altarpiece (detail): The Temptation of St Anthony, *Matthias Grünewald*]

hands, and they listened to what the Church told them.

Many churches commissioned paintings for their altars. These altarpieces showed incidents from the life and death of Jesus and often portrayed saints as examples of how to live a good life. Matthias Grünewald, a 15th-century German painter, had strong religious feelings and his paintings express emotions forcefully. Grünewald's altarpiece (see page opposite) dwelt on the horrors awaiting the wicked on their arrival in hell.

Judgement day

The passage from life to death has always been a great mystery. Various cultures tell fascinating stories about it, many of them remarkably similar. Like Christians, Muslims believe that there will be a day of judgement, when Allah will ask people to give an account of the way they have lived. The Muslim holy book, the Koran, says that the blessed shall recline on jewelled couches and be waited on, whilst the damned shall dwell amidst scorching winds and boiling water. It is said that Mohammed had a

▲ *This is a scene from Mohammed's mystical vision. Riding on the heavenly horse Buaq, and guided by the archangel Gabriel, he rose through the layers of the created world to confront the 'unseen infinite'. After this event, many people were converted to the faith of Islam. This Persian miniature shows angels surrounding the* Prophet. *Which one do you think might be Gabriel? Compare this painting with the Indian miniature on page 11. Note the intricate and colourful designs in both. Mohammed's face is veiled because it is forbidden to show his face in a painting.* [Ascent of the Prophet Mohammed to Heaven, *Persian miniature*]

mystical vision in which, guided by the archangel Gabriel, he journeyed through the real world to see the 'unseen infinite' – the afterlife. You can see Mohammed's mystical journey illustrated in the Persian miniature on page 41.

The ancient Greeks believed in an afterlife (called the Underworld, or Hades) at the centre of the earth. Their dead were also judged according to their deeds on earth. The good went to the happy Elysian fields, the wicked to a terrible place called Tartarus. Rivers that flowed underground in Greece were thought to lead to the land of the dead.

The ferryman

The Greeks believed that there was an underground river, called the Styx, which formed the border between the world of the living and the Underworld. Dead souls had to ask the official ferryman, Charon, to take them across the river. He was a difficult, bad-tempered old man. A dead soul who could not pay for the journey was left to wander aimlessly along the banks of the river forever. The

The pictures in this chapter describe different versions of the afterlife. See if you can find some more examples. Look at the differences between some of the world religions, such as Buddhism, Christianity, Hinduism, Islam. Look at the beliefs of more localized cultures – American Indians and African tribes for example. Which beliefs are shared by two or more religions?

Greeks put coins into the mouths of their dead so that Charon would be paid to take them across the Styx.

Joachim Patenier, who painted the picture of Charon on the page opposite, lived in Antwerp in the 15th century. He specialized in painting landscapes with fantastic scenery, using very cool colours with strong blues in the distance. The people and animals in his paintings were almost always tiny. Sometimes he employed other artists to paint them for him while he concentrated on the landscape.

Preserved bodies

For the ancient Egyptians, the afterlife was another version of the Egypt they already knew. They thought that if they could preserve a person's dead body, then that person was not really dead and could make the journey to the afterlife. The dead person's liver, lungs and other internal organs were cut out and preserved in separate storage jars, called canopic jars. Only the heart remained in the body, so that it could be weighed in the afterlife. The body was dried out to prevent it from decaying, then rubbed

◄ The Greek ferryman Charon takes a dead soul across the River Styx to the Underworld. The left-hand bank is a peaceful place, with images of tranquillity and 'goodness', while the right-hand bank is a fearsome place. Look at the two-headed monster with the long tail lurking by the tunnelled gateway, and the dreadful scene on top. This is a strange inhospitable landscape which we look down on from a high view point, as if we were a bird or a god. How does the artist make us feel as if we are on the edge of the world?
[Charon, Joachim Patenier]

Boat trip to the afterlife

For a king, priest or noble of ancient Egypt, the journey to the afterlife began with a boat trip. The mummified body of the dead person was placed under a canopy on the boat. Guarded by two mourners, it was carried along the river Nile to a tomb that had been painted, then filled with things to accompany the dead person into the afterlife. This journey was often depicted in wall paintings.

Funeral boats were decorated to look like the one used by the sun god Ra on his journey through the underworld. The sides of the boats were painted green to signify new life. Craftsmen made small models of the funeral boats, which were put into the tombs to enable the dead souls to continue their journey.

Many museums have Egyptian mummies in their collections. You may also be lucky enough to see small models of the funeral boats.

with ointment and wrapped in bandages. In this state it was now a mummy.

The mummified body was placed in a coffin. Rich people could afford many-layered coffins, one inside the other. Artists were employed to decorate them with magic

Canopic jars

The Egyptians used four special containers, called canopic jars, to store the body's organs while the rest of the body was mummified for its journey to the afterlife. The lids of the jars were modelled in the shapes of four Egyptian gods, known as the sons of Horus. The gods each protected different organs. The jackal-headed god, Duamutef, protected the stomach. Qebehsenuef had a hawk's head and guarded the intestines. Hapy the dog-headed baboon watched over the lungs. The human-headed god, Imsety, guarded the liver.

Over the years, canopic jars were made from different materials. The Egyptians had been making containers by baking clay from before 4000 BC, but by 2500 BC they had developed the technology to hollow out and shape stone into bowls and jars.

Some time after this, they learnt how to shape molten glass into sophisticated vessels. Copper ores were used to give the glass a distinctive blue colour.

A ferocious protector

The tombs of Egyptian kings were protected by statues of gods in the guise of ferocious animals. Their job was to frighten off the king's enemies as he travelled to the afterlife. Make your own fierce protector out of clay or plasticine. Ours is made of plasticine.

What you need
- ball of coloured plasticine or self-hardening clay about the size of a tennis ball
- piece of old board to work on
- paint and varnish

What you do
1 Decide on the animal you would like to be your protector. It could be a fierce version of your own pet, or you could invent your own dragon or monster.
2 Model your animal. Exaggerate some features, such as the teeth and claws.
3 If you are modelling with plasticine, use different coloured pieces. If you are using self-hardening clay, paint and varnish your animal.

◀ This wall painting from an Egyptian tomb shows Anubis, the god of embalming, laying out a dead person. Anubis is easily recognized by his jackal's head. It is he who guides the dead through the first stage of the journey to the afterlife. See how many different patterns there are in the painting. [Anubis embalming a mummy, from a tomb in the Valley of the Kings, Egypt]

spells and pictures of the gods of the afterlife for protection. The dead person's portrait was painted on the outside. As Egyptian tombs have been excavated over the years, many coffins containing well-preserved mummies have been uncovered.

We know so much about the Egyptians because the walls of important tombs were covered with paintings.

The hot dry climate of Egypt was ideal for wall painting. The colours could be painted straight on to the dry plaster without fear that damp weather would ruin the surface. Some scenes described the journey of the dead. Others showed everyday life in the real world. These ordinary scenes were to help the dead person feel at home in the afterlife.

About the artists

(Only some of the artists are listed below. Many of the works of art in this book are by artists whose names we no longer know.)

BENTON, Thomas Hart (1889-1975) Benton was born in Missouri where he also spent the last 40 years of his life. He is best known for his large-scale murals. He painted scenes of rural America in flowing rhythmic shapes. Benton lived in Paris for a while, and during the 1920s and 1930s taught in New York City, where the American artist Jackson Pollock was one of his pupils.

BROWN, Ford Madox (1821-1893) This English artist was born in Calais, France, and studied in Belgium, Paris and Rome. He gave painting lessons after he came to live in London and was influenced by the ideas of his pupil, Dante Gabriel Rossetti, an important member of the Pre-Raphaelite group of artists.

CARAVAGGIO, Michelangelo Merisi da (1573-1610) Caravaggio's earliest works were still-life subjects, but he later painted many religious pictures. His works were full of drama, strong lights and shadows. He was a violent man and always in trouble with the police. He even murdered his opponent after they had quarrelled in a tennis match.

DELACROIX, Eugène (1798-1863) Delacroix's brilliant use of colour and his dramatic subjects caused him to be labelled a Romantic painter. He was very impressed with the freshness of English painting of the period, and tried to paint in a similar way. Some of his finest works are the large decorations that he made for many public buildings in France.

DELANEY, Joseph (1904-1991) Delaney was born and died in Knoxville, Tennessee, but he spent most of his life in New York City. He was a student of Thomas Hart Benton (see above). Delaney was the first African-American artist to receive a retrospective exhibition at a major southern university – at Knoxville in 1970.

GAUGUIN, Paul (1848-1903) The French artist Gauguin was born in Paris but spent some of his childhood in Peru. He started his working life as a stockbroker, but in 1883 he gave up his job to become a full-time artist. He later separated from his family as a result of financial problems. He was inspired by non-European art and an exotic way of life. He died in the Marquesas Islands in the South Pacific.

GILLE, Sieghard (b. 1941) Gille, a contemporary painter and printmaker, is from the former German Democratic Republic. He is considered an important artist of the 1960s and '70s, but since the Berlin Wall came down in 1989 many former East German artists, including Gille, have had difficulty making their name in the West and have lost the standing they once had in the East.

GOZZOLI, Benozzo (c.1421-97) Like many other artists of the Italian Renaissance, Gozzoli painted murals for Italian churches and palaces. Although they were of religious subjects, they seemed very worldly. He worked mainly in Florence.

GRÜNEWALD, Matthias (c.1470-1528) Little is known of the life of Grünewald (whose real name was Mathis Gothart-Nithart), but we do know that for some time he was court painter to the Elector of Mainz. He was dismissed from this post because of his sympathies with the new religious movement of Lutherism. He seems to have died very poor. His most famous work is the Isenheim Altarpiece which is now in the museum at Colmar in France.

MUNAKATA, Shiko (1903-1975) Munakata lived in Tokyo for most of his life, but he travelled widely in Europe. He was particularly moved by the work of Vincent van Gogh. Munakata was a painter and printmaker, working in the traditional Japanese medium of woodcut. During the war his studio and nearly all his work were destroyed in an air raid. 'The faster I work,' he once said, 'the better the results, but when I finish so swiftly, I'm left with a sort of sadness.'

PAOLO, Giovanni di (d. 1482) A leading painter in Siena, Italy, in the 15th century. At this time, known as the Renaissance, painting was going through great changes. Giovanni di Paolo resisted these changes and continued to paint in the old tradition.

PATENIER, Joachim (d.c.1524) Although many of the great museums of the world own pictures by Patenier, very little is known about his life. He was registered in 1515 as a member of the Antwerp guild of painters. Sometimes his figures were painted by someone else while he concentrated on the landscapes.

RAPHAEL (Raffaello Sanzio) of Urbino (1483-1520) Raphael was renowned for being gracious and charming. He was born in Urbino, Italy, but his greatest work was done in Florence and Rome. He was employed by two popes and he made famous portraits of both of them. He died when he was only 37.

REMBRANDT, Harmensz van Rijn (1606-69) The son of a miller, Rembrandt became a successful painter in Amsterdam, Holland. His painting and printmaking were usually characterized by areas of strong light and deep shadows, which created a powerful emotional effect. He was forced to reduce his extravagant lifestyle when he was made bankrupt.

ROWLANDSON, Thomas (1756-1827) A fine draughtsman, Rowlandson was born in London but studied in Paris. He gambled away his fortune early on in his life, after which he earned his living selling his prints. He specialized in capturing the bustle of ordinary people going about their lives. His drawings are full of life and humour.

SEGAL, George (b. 1924) Born in New York City, Segal was a chicken farmer before he became a professional artist. He stresses the loneliness and emptiness in human lives. His technique is to cover a person with plaster bandages until they dry, then cut the bandages open to let the person out. Finally he puts the plaster mould together again.

TURNER, Joseph Mallord William (1775-1851) Turner, one of the most famous English artists, was born in London. He exhibited his first work at the Royal Academy when he was only 15 years old. A successful painter throughout his life, he became Professor of Perspective at the Royal Academy. Turner loved most of all to paint all kinds of weather, particularly when this was combined with ships and water. When he died, Turner left over 20,000 works of art.

YOSHITOSHI, Tsukioka (1839-92) One of the greatest Japanese printmakers and also a highly skilled draughtsman. He was particularly interested in historical and heroic subjects. After the opening up of Japan to the West, Yoshitoshi became influenced by western drawing styles.

Acknowledgements

National Gallery, London, 4; The British Museum, London, 8; Hirshhorn Museum and Sculpture Garden, Smithsonian Institution, Gift of Joseph H. Hirschhorn, 1966/photo: Lee Stalsworth, 14; Werner Forman Archive, 16; Martyn Gregory, 17; The Japanese Gallery/photo: Patrick Conner, 26; The British Museum, London, 28; Collection of the Mingeikan, 29; Teylers Museum, Haarlem, Netherlands, 35.

All other pictures are from the Bridgeman Art Library, courtesy of the following: Birmingham City Museums and Art Gallery, 6; National Museum of American Art, Smithsonian Institution, 7; Bluett & Sons, London, 10; Victoria and Albert Museum, London, 11; Victoria and Albert Museum, London, 12; Private Collection/© DACS 1996, 13; British Library, London, 18; Harry S. Truman Library and Museum, Independence, MO/© Estate of Hart Benton/DACS, London/ VAGA, New York 1996, 19; Chicago Historical Society, 20; Vatican Museums and Galleries, Rome, 22; British Library, London, 24; Palazzo Medici-Riccardi, Florence, 25; Louvre, Paris, 31; Santa Maria del Popolo, Rome, 32; Prado, Madrid, 34; National Gallery, London, 37; National Gallery London/Topham Picturepoint, 38; Unterlinden Museum, Colmar, France, 40; British Library, London, 41; Prado, Madrid, 42; Valley of the Kings, Thebes, Egypt/Lauros-Giraudon, 44.

Index